CONTENTS

EQUIPMENT AND MATERIALS

This book describes activities which use the following:

Adhesive tape, double-sided
Adhesives (PVA, cold water paste)
Apron
Black colours (inks, paints, pens)
Bowl
Camera
Card (white)
Cellophane sheets (or acetate or plastic)
Compasses
Cooking fat
Drinking straws
Ebony stain
Fabrics – plain, cotton
– printed, coloured
Felt-tip pens
Iron
Leaves
Light-scope
Magazine (for pictures)
Magnifying glass
Paintbrush
Paints – acryclic paints
– oil paints
– powder paints
– water-colour paints
Palette (or plate)
Paper – black paper
– blotting paper
– coloured paper
– sugar paper (various colours)
– tissue paper (various colours)
– white paper
Pebbles (or marbles)
Pencil
Plant materials
Plant supports
Prism (triangular, glass)
Rubber bands
Rubber gloves
Ruler
Saucepan (old)
Scissors
String (thin)
Sunglasses
Washing-up liquid
Water
Wax crayons
Wood (an old branch, small twigs)
Wood ash

INTRODUCTION

All the colours of the rainbow are contained in the white light of the Sun, and because our eyes are sensitive to different colours in light we can see these colours all around us. We can see many different colours, but not every animal can see colour. Horses, dogs, cats and cows see the world in black, grey and white. Reptiles, birds, insects and fish can see in colour, like human beings.

When we look at different objects, we see them in different colours. This is because when light shines on an object only some of the colour in light is reflected back into our eyes and the other colours are absorbed by the object. A red car reflects back the red colour in light, so it looks red. White things reflect all the colours in light; black things absorb all the colours – they reflect no light.

Colour has many uses. You will learn about these as you work through this book. In nature, animals and plants use colour. Sometimes they use it to camouflage themselves — they hide from enemies. Sometimes they use bright colours to attract attention. We use colours too. Red often can be a warning colour. It is used in traffic lights to stop the cars. It is used in flags on beaches to tell us not to swim.

Did you know that light travels in

waves? Think of the ripples that form when you drop a pebble in still water. The waves spread out in rings from their source and are different lengths, or wavelengths. Our eyes are sensitive to the different wavelengths in light, and so we can see different colours. But we can only detect the light rays in the middle of the band of wavelengths. We call this the visible spectrum. Ultra-violet rays have shorter wavelengths, and we cannot see them. They are used in medicine and X-rays. Infra-red rays have longer wavelengths, and are used in night photography and electronics. The remote control units of televisions and video sets work using infra-red light.

By following the investigations in this book you will learn something about the science of colour. At the start of each section there are some scientific ideas to be explored. A scientist looks at ideas and tries to discover if they are always true, and will also investigate to see if they can be *disproved.* You will be working like a scientist. A scientist is curious and wants to find out about the world in which we live. A scientist tests ideas, makes investigations and experiments, and tries to explain what has happened. Your results may be surprising or unexpected, and you may find that you will need to carry out a new investigation, or test a new idea.

You will also be an artist. You will be using colour in the art activities that are included in each section. Through working with both colour and the various art materials and techniques, you will make discoveries about the nature of colour and how colour can be used. Your finished pieces of art will be a record of your scientific findings.

COLOURS IN LIGHT

White light contains all the colours in the visible spectrum – red, orange, yellow, green, blue, indigo, and violet. Each colour has a different wavelength. If a beam of light passes through a glass surface at an angle it bends (it is refracted). If it passes through the sides of a triangular prism it is bent twice and the different light wavelengths are separated. You can see the colours of the rainbow.

The colours of the spectrum can be seen when sunlight passes through raindrops.

White light contains all the colours in the visible spectrum.

Read about Sir Isaac Newton, a 17th-century scientist. He noticed that when a beam of sunlight shone through a crack in the shutters of his study window onto a glass prism, it made a band of bright colours. He wondered where the colours came from.

Rainbow art

You will need: white paper, wax crayons, ebony stain, a paintbrush, an iron, some newspapers.

1. Draw and colour a rainbow picture using wax crayons in the colours of the spectrum. Remember to use your crayons in the right order – red, orange, yellow, green, blue, indigo, violet.

2. Crumple your picture into a ball, then smooth it out again. Spread the newspaper on the table for protection. Brush the ebony stain firmly into the cracks of the crayon picture. The creases can then be removed by ironing your picture between two sheets of clean paper.

3. "Rainbow face". Notice how the ink has entered into the cracks to create an interesting pattern. This art technique is called paper batik.

SEEING COLOUR

The human eye is able to detect differences in the wavelengths of light. Different cells in the retina at the back of the eye are sensitive to the red, green and blue colours in light. The retina can also detect black and white so that when you go out at night and there is little light, you can still see things, but they appear to be black, white and grey.

Go outside after dark. What colours can you see? Look again in the daylight and notice how the colours have changed. Ask a doctor or a nurse what tests they might use to discover whether a person is colour-blind. A colour-blind person cannot distinguish between certain colours, for example red and green.
Read about Georges Seurat, the famous French artist. He developed a technique called "pointilism" — painting with small dots. He also studied the science of colour and optics, the science of vision.

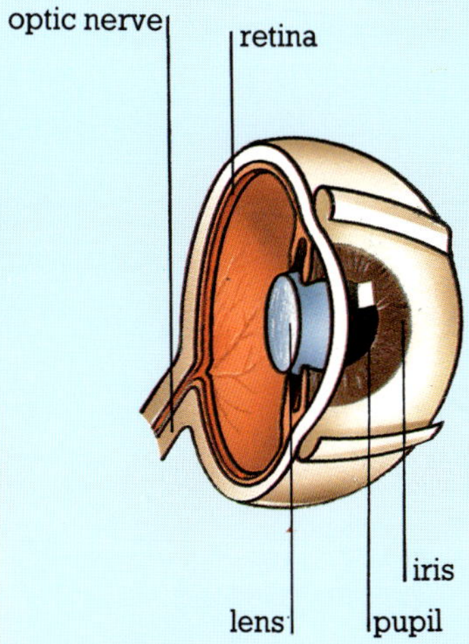

This drawing shows the parts of the eye.

Painting with dots

You will need: white paper, drinking straws (or a plant support), red, green and blue paints.

1. Draw a circle on a piece of paper. Use a small piece of straw (or stick) to mark the circumference with green dots of paint. Draw a triangle inside the circle and outline this with dots too.

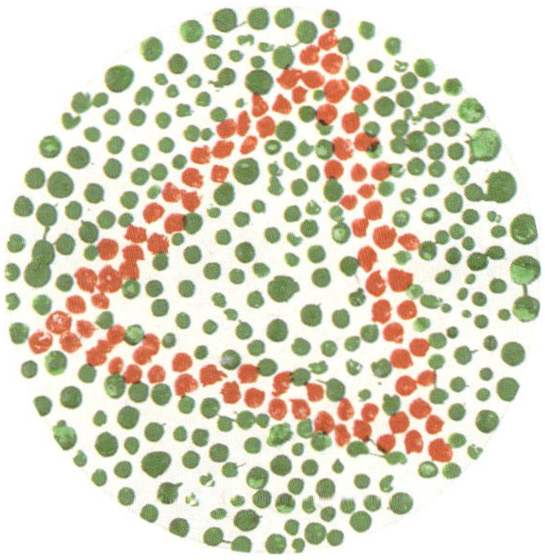

2. Fill in the triangle with red dots and the background with green dots. Some people find it difficult to distinguish between red and green. Ask your friends if they can see the triangle.

3. "Fish". Draw a picture using dots. Use only the red, green and blue paints. Notice here how the impression of purple is given where the red and blue dots are close together.

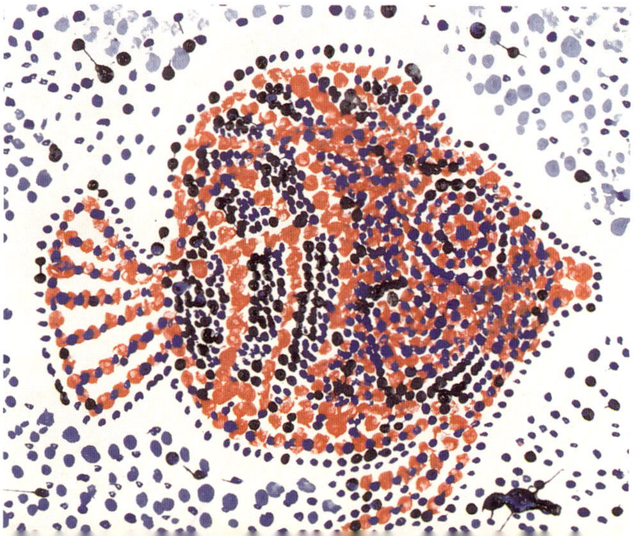

Background colour affects the colours you see

You will need: sugar paper in a range of colours, scissors.

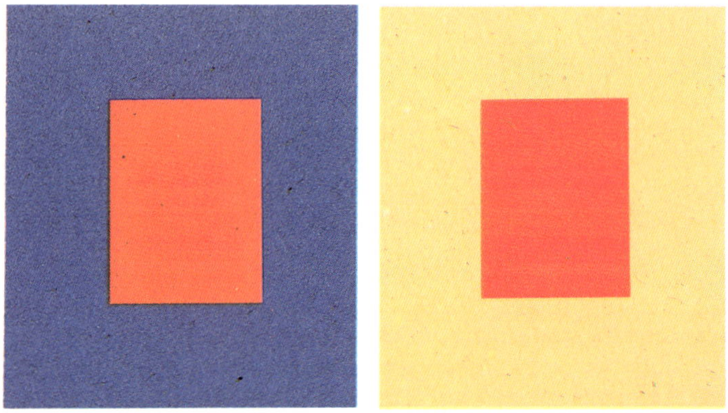

1. Have a look at these pairs of rectangles. The small inner rectangle appears to be a different colour from the one next to it because it has been placed on a different background. They are really the same colour.

2. Experiment with your paper. Cut two small rectangles of one colour and place them on two contrasting background colours. Do they look different?

MIXING LIGHT COLOURS

Red, green and blue are the primary light colours. By mixing these colours we can make other colours. Red and green light mixed together make yellow, green and blue light together make cyan (a turquoise colour), and red and blue light make magenta (a deep, purplish red). Yellow, cyan and magenta are secondary colours of light.

When the three primary light colours – red, green and blue – are mixed together in equal proportions they re-form into white light again.

Look at a colour television screen through a magnifying glass. The picture is made up of areas of red, green and blue. Your brain mixes the colours so you see many different colours. Use a light-scope to look closely at a colour magazine picture. What colours do you see?

Colour spinners

You will need: a pair of compasses, white card, a pencil, ruler, thin string, red, blue and green felt-tip pens, scissors.

1. Draw and cut out several circles from the white card. Colour the circles in different combinations of colours. Use only two colours at a time.

2. Colour one circle red, blue and green in equal proportions.

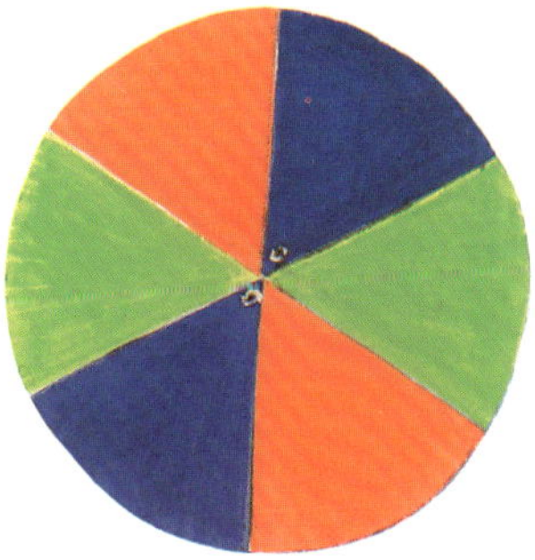

4. Make two holes on either side of the centre of the card circle (approximately 1cm apart). Thread a piece of string through the holes, and tie it in a loop.

3. Draw and cut out a circle with a radius of 7cm. Draw concentric circles, 1cm apart, and colour alternate rings red, blue and green, as shown. Colour each remaining ring in a combination of the two colours which lie on either side of the ring.

5. Relax and tighten the string to spin your disc.

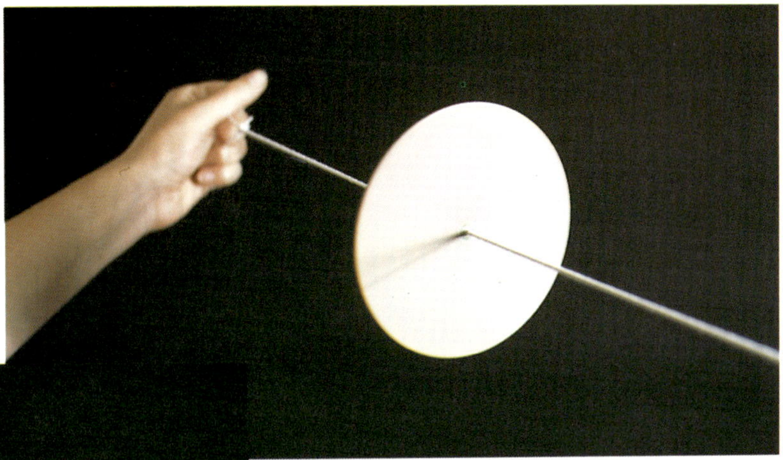

Red, green and blue disc

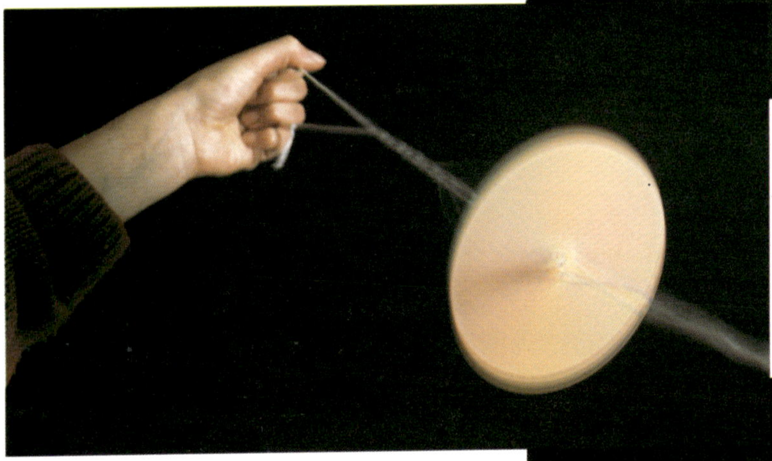

Red and blue disc

"Rainbow colours"

Do the colours bend more easily if the circles are divided into eight segments instead of only two?

Make some spinners in different designs. What do you think you will see?

FILTERING LIGHT

If you look through a coloured filter (a transparent coloured sheet of plastic cellophane or glass) the colours that you see will change. This is because the filter will only allow light of its own colour to pass through.

A red filter will only let red light through. If you look at a red object through a red filter it becomes pale because the red light has travelled through the filter.

Put on a pair of sunglasses. Notice how the colours that you see change. Sunglasses protect your eyes from bright sunlight. They filter out the glare. When you visit the theatre, notice how coloured filters are used for stage lighting.

WARNING: NEVER LOOK DIRECTLY AT THE SUN THROUGH A FILTER OR SUNGLASSES, AS IT IS DANGEROUS AND CAN DAMAGE YOUR EYES.

Looking at a strawberry through a red filter.

Using colour filters

You will need: white paper, felt-tip pens, some coloured cellophane, plastic or acetate sheets.

1. A test sheet. Draw a multi-coloured pattern of shapes on white paper, using felt-tip pens. Study your design carefully through the different coloured filters. Do the colours disappear? Do the colours change? Keep a record of which colours are affected by each filter.

2. "The train". Use the information you have discovered to make a disappearing picture.

3. Notice here how the green colour shows up darkly through the red filter and the yellow and orange colours disappear.

4. Here, with the blue filter, the train has changed completely.

WARNING: NEVER HOLD PLASTIC OR CELLOPHANE RIGHT UP TO YOUR FACE.

Colour weaving

You will need: two card strips (approximately 20 × 4cm), coloured cellophane, double-sided adhesive tape.

1. Stick a strip of adhesive tape, 16cm long, along one edge of a card strip. Cut four cellophane strips, 4cm wide, in red, yellow, blue and green. Stick them side by side to the tape. Weave four cross-strips of cellophane in and out alternately, as shown.

2. Trim the first strips and attach these to the second card strip at the base.

3. "Colour square". Here the coloured strips overlap each other in both directions. Notice how two layers of the same colour deepen the colour. How many different shades of colour can you see?

PIGMENT

Pigmentation is the natural colouring of plants and minerals, and of the skins of people and animals.

Pigments (tiny particles of colour) also give colour to man-made paints and dyes. Paint colours are not so pure as light colours. You cannot mix paint colour to obtain a yellow. Yellow, red and blue are the primary colours in paint.

Pigments reflect their own colour and absorb the rest. When you mix paints or pigments, different colours are absorbed. If all the colours of the spectrum are mixed together all the colours will be absorbed and only black will remain.

Make a collection of objects and sort them by colour. Look very closely at each object. Is the object naturally coloured? Has the surface been painted, or is the colour part of the material with which the object has been made? Visit an art gallery and notice how different artists use colour in their paintings. Look carefully at one painting. Is it brightly coloured? Has the artist only used a limited range of colours?

Yellow, red and blue are the primary colours in paint.

Mixing paint colours

You will need: red, yellow and blue powder paint, a palette or plate, a paintbrush, water.

1. With a little water, mix some red and yellow paint together in equal proportions. Repeat with the blue and yellow, then the red and blue. What colour is made if you mix all three colours together?

2. A colour chart. Make your own chart to show the primary (red, yellow and blue) and secondary (orange, green and purple) paint colours. In the chart shown, the secondary colours have been mixed together also to produce the tertiary colours, browns and greys.

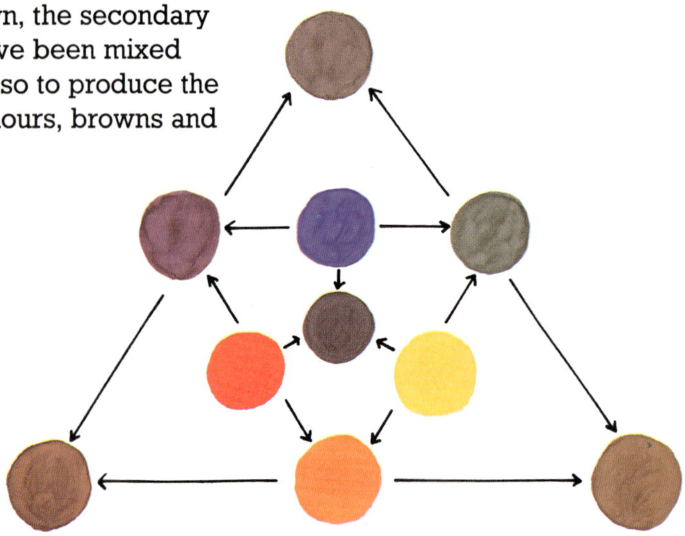

3. Experiment to see what colour you obtain if you mix a primary colour with a secondary colour, such as red with orange. See how many different colours you can make by mixing just the three primary colours in different proportions. The variety is endless!

"Streptocarpus". Try to paint a picture of a plant using only the three primary colours. Can you mix the right amount of colour to echo exactly the colours of the plant? Does the background colour affect your painting?

How black is black?

You will need: different black colours such as pens, paints and inks, strips of blotting paper (or other absorbent paper), a bowl of water.

Is the black in pens and inks really black? You can use chromatography to test this.

1. Choose a selection of your own different black colours. Here a felt-tip pen, a handwriting pen, paint and black ink are being tested. Near one end of a strip of absorbent paper, draw and fill in a circle of black. Try to make the spots the same size for each black being tested. Suspend the strips over a bowl of water so that the edges of the paper just touch the water.

2. The water will be absorbed and move up the paper. The colours in the spots will be carried along the paper by the water and will separate. You will be able to see which colours were mixed together to make black.

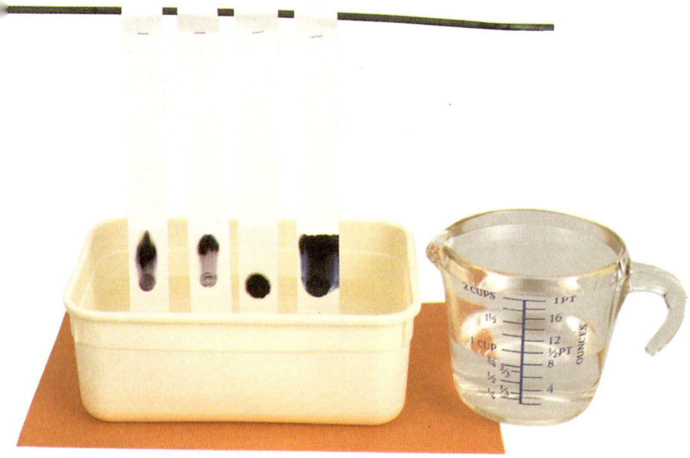

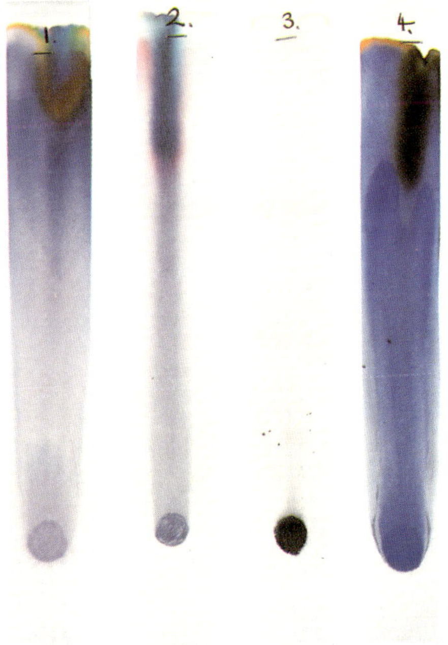

COLOUR MEDIUMS

Artists use colour in a variety of different mediums. Some colour mediums are wet, such as paints, inks and dyes. Other colour mediums are dry art materials. These include pencils, crayons, chalks and pastels.

Paint pigments are used in different mediums which bind the pigments together. This affects the style of painting, and how the artist works.

Water-colours are bound with a water-soluble medium such as gum arabic, and they dry quickly.

Acrylic paints are made by mixing the pigment with a PVA (poly vinyl acetate) medium. These can be worked thickly, and dry very quickly with a shiny finish.

Oil paints are pigments mixed with oil. They are bought as thick paint in tubes and can be thinned with linseed oil or white spirit. They dry very slowly.

Look at a coloured wooden toy. Why would it not be sensible to colour a wooden model with coloured crayons?
Study a picture of an illuminated manuscript. Monks in the early Middle Ages decorated their books with fine water-colour paintings, often the first capital letter on a page and the margins of the pages. You could try to decorate your initials in a similar way.

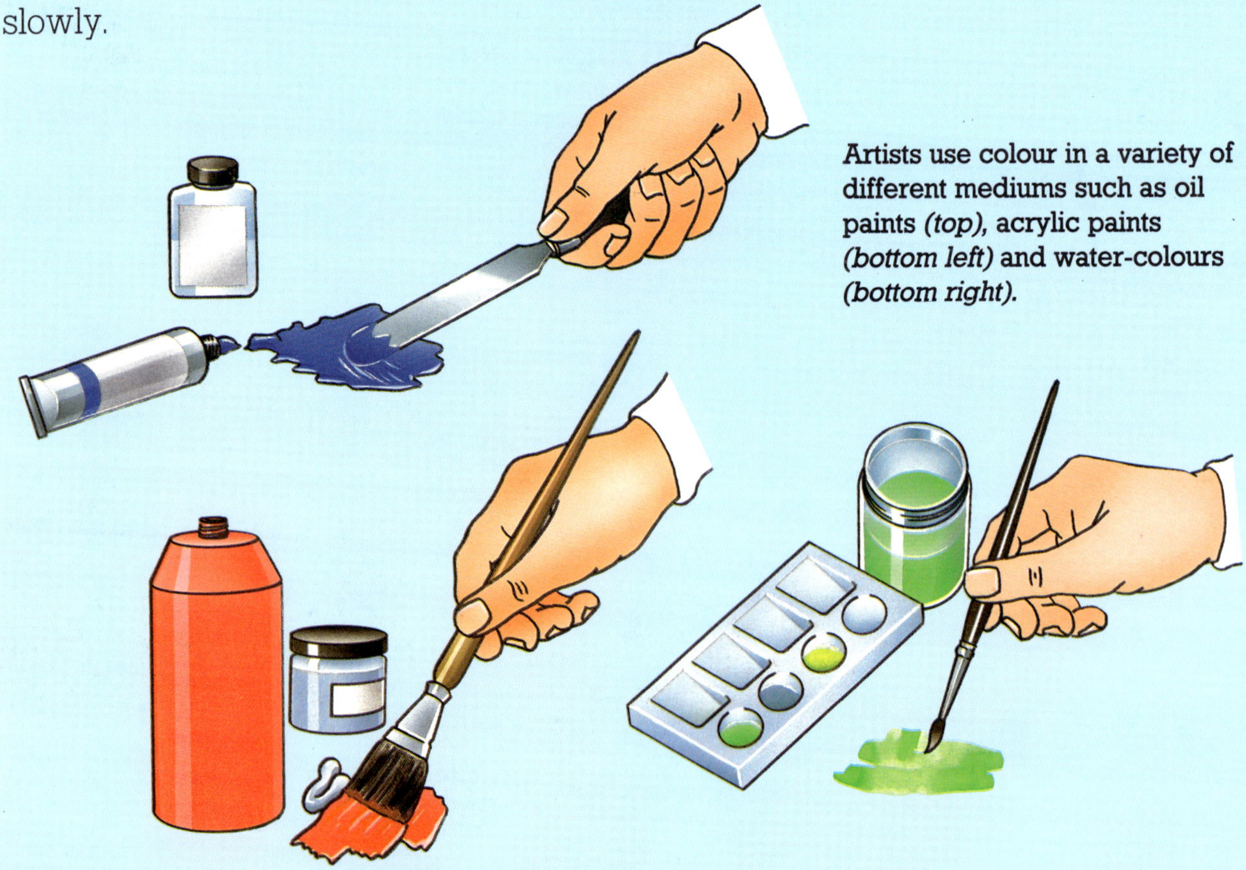

Artists use colour in a variety of different mediums such as oil paints *(top)*, acrylic paints *(bottom left)* and water-colours *(bottom right)*.

Artists' colours – a test chart

You will need: a small quantity of colours in different wet and dry mediums.

1. Test each colour medium separately and make a chart of your results.

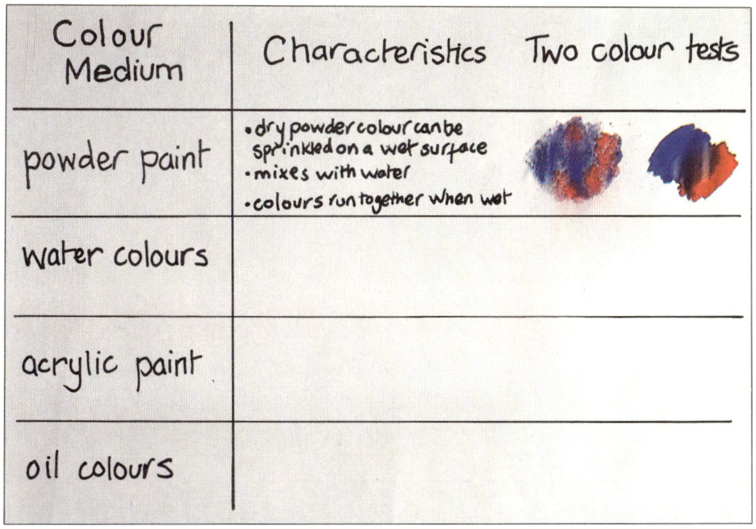

2. Think of some questions to ask about each medium. Here are some ideas. Wet colours: Do the colours run together? Do they dry quickly? What can you use to apply the colour? How do you thin the colour? Dry colours: Are they soft? Do they smudge? Do they blend together easily?

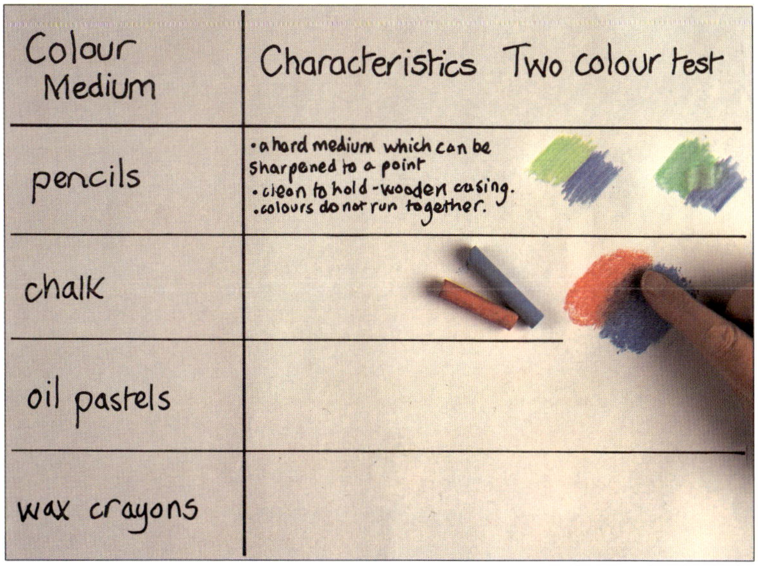

"Fun with colour". Using powder colour and coloured papers.

"St Paul's", using acrylic paints. These can be applied thickly and interesting textures can be created.

COLOUR IN NATURE

Look at a garden, a field, the sky, the sea. You will see many colours. The colours you see will change as the light changes. In bright sunlight the colours are more brilliant. On a dark day, everything seems more grey.

Throughout the year, too, the colours in nature change as the plants, flowers and trees change with the seasons. Every plant, flower and animal has its own colouring. Studying their colours will help you to recognize them.

Spring

Summer

Autumn

Find a stone. How many different colours can you see in it? Do the colours change if you make it wet? Some flowers are red, for example, roses. Can you think of a flower for each colour of the spectrum?

Throughout the year the colour of many plants and trees changes with the seasons.

Camouflage

Some animals have colours that make them difficult to be seen in their natural surroundings. This is called camouflage. It helps them hide and keep safe from their enemies.

Sometimes camouflage helps animals to stalk their prey and get close without being seen. A polar bear is difficult to see against the arctic ice.

Leaf collage

You will need: a collection of leaves, PVA glue diluted with water to make a glaze, a paintbrush, paper.

1. Brush glaze over the surface of the paper and arrange your design of leaves. (This will be very sticky.) Coat each leaf with glaze and leave to dry.

2. The glaze will become shiny, and the leaves will be preserved as the air has been excluded. What do you think will happen to the leaves you have picked, but do not use?

3. Compare the two pictures. What do you notice about the colours of the leaves?

Camouflage experiment

You will need: an animal picture (from an old magazine), different coloured paper.

Cut out your chosen animal picture. Place it on different coloured background papers to see which gives the most camouflage. You could try to create better camouflage by adding some crayon details.

1. Lion. Which background offers the lion better camouflage?

2. Zebra. Why is it difficult to see a zebra against a background of black and white? Would it be possible to camouflage this zebra even more with the black and white crayons?

COLOUR FROM NATURE

Long ago early painters obtained their colours from the materials around them. Reds and yellows came from the rocks and earth, blacks and greys from the ash and wood of their fires. Early hunters painted pictures of wild animals on the walls of their caves. The paintings were made using a mixture of coloured earths and animal fats.

Dyes, too, can be obtained from nature. Before synthetic (man-made) dyes were invented, people used plant juices to dye their clothes. Some vegetable dyes are colourfast – the colours will not wash out – but most wash out easily unless a special fixer, called a mordant, is added.

Why do you think instructions for washing clothes advise you to separate light and dark colours? Have you ever spilt ink on the floor or a drink on your clothes? How difficult was it to wipe away the marks?

Dyes can be made by boiling plant material such as tea, beetroot, walnuts and onions.

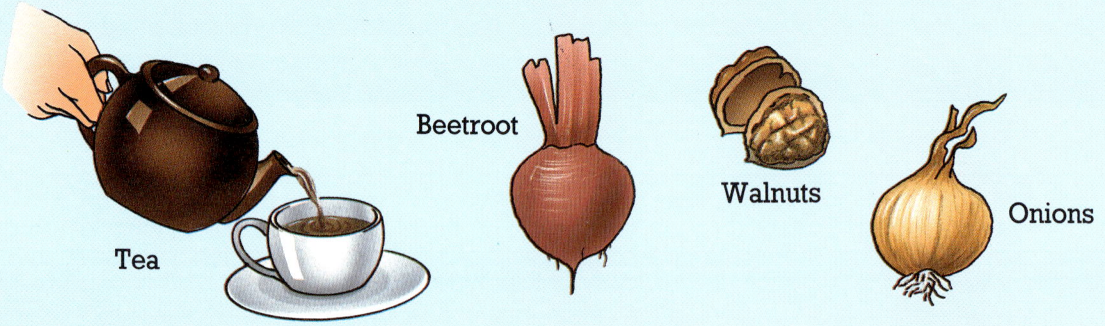

Pictures from wood

You will need: a piece of burnt wood (charcoal), some paper, a piece of broken branch, ash from a wood fire, cooking fat, a palette knife.

1. Find a piece of broken branch. Use your home-made charcoal to make a sketch of the branch. Look carefully at the wood and notice how many colours there are.

2. You can experiment with cold wood ash too. A mixture of ash with a little cooking fat gives an interesting texture for art work, and can be applied with a palette knife.

Make your own natural dyes

You will need: plant materials, (roots, leaves, fruits or bark), an old saucepan, water.

Ask a grown-up to help you. Put your chosen plant material into your saucepan with some water. Boil the plant material until the colour moves from the plant to the water.

Leave the mixture to cool, then drain off the coloured solution. Very often the colours obtained are shades of yellow and brown.

1. Boiling onion skins. These give a strong yellow dye which will give a permanent stain.

WARNING: REMEMBER THAT SOME PLANTS ARE PROTECTED SPECIES AND MUST NOT BE TAKEN FROM THE WILD.

ALSO, SOME PLANTS ARE POISONOUS SO CHECK WITH AN ADULT BEFORE PICKING ANYTHING.

2. Different dyes obtained from nature. From left to right: onion skins, laurel bark, dandelion roots, beetroot, tea, walnut shells, heather, lilac leaves.

Tie-and-dye

You will need: a bowl, your coloured natural dyes, small pebbles or marbles, rubber bands, string, some pieces of cotton fabric, rubber gloves, an apron.

1. Tie your fabric in different ways. You can make knots, or tie it tightly with string as shown.

2. Here marbles are being placed in the fabric and held in position with rubber bands. Twist several rubber bands around each marble as tightly as you can.

3. Put on your apron and your rubber gloves to protect you and your clothes. Choose a coloured dye and pour it into a bowl. Dip the fabric into the dye and push it down under the surface.

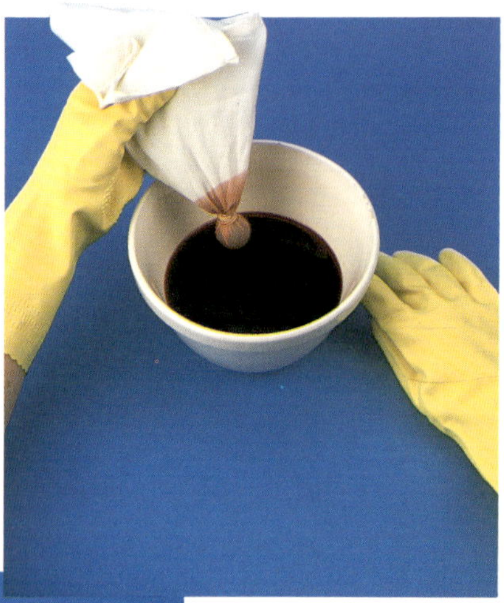

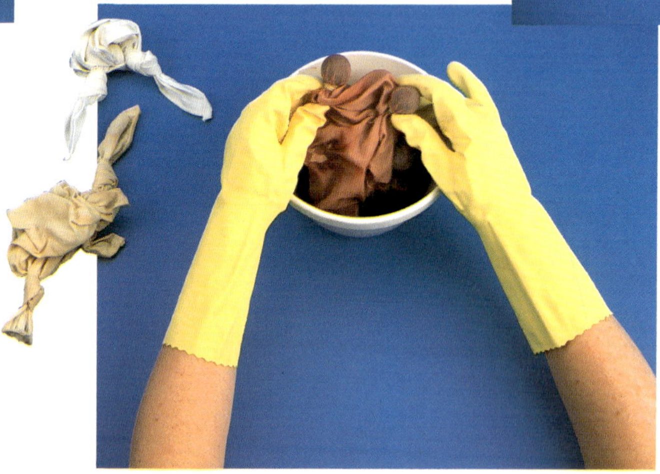

4. Allow the dye to soak into the fabric for a short while (about two minutes), then lift it out and leave it to dry. (The knotted square on the left has been soaked in onion dye).

5. When the fabric is completely dry, remove the rubber bands and open it out. Notice how the rubber bands protected the fabric from the dye giving an interesting pattern. Ask a grown-up to help you iron your fabric.

6. "Flower design". White crayon drawing, painted with natural dyes.

COLOURS AND FEELINGS

If you bend the spectrum of colours round into a circle you will have a colour wheel. The colour wheel can help you choose colours that go well together. We call these colours harmonious. They are found next to each other on the colour wheel.

Colours which lie opposite one another on the colour wheel are called complementary colours. These dazzle the eye when they are put side by side.

Colours can affect our feelings. Harmonious colours put together are calming, but complementary colours startle and excite the senses.

A room decorated in pinks and reds feels warm, whereas a blue-coloured room feels cold. Why do you think the quiet reading room in a library is not painted in bright complementary colours?

Look at a large street advertisement. Have bright, contrasting colours been used to attract the eye?

A dazzling pattern in contrasting colours.

A colour wheel

1. Make your own colour wheel. Oil pastels have been used for this wheel.

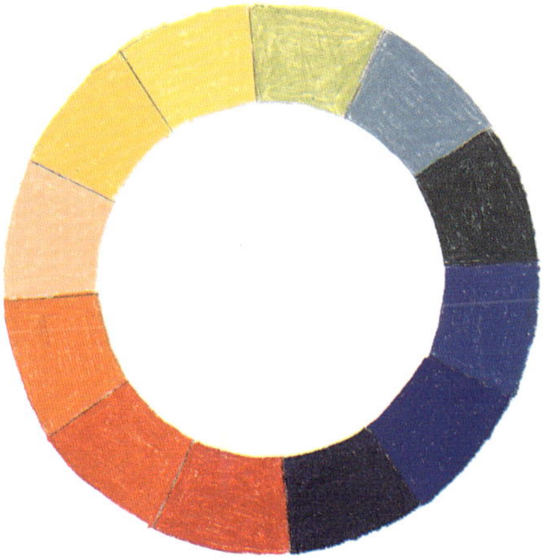

2. Experiment with pairs of colours: harmonious colours and complementary colours. Which pairs of colours do you like together?

3. Which colours would you choose to decorate your bedroom?

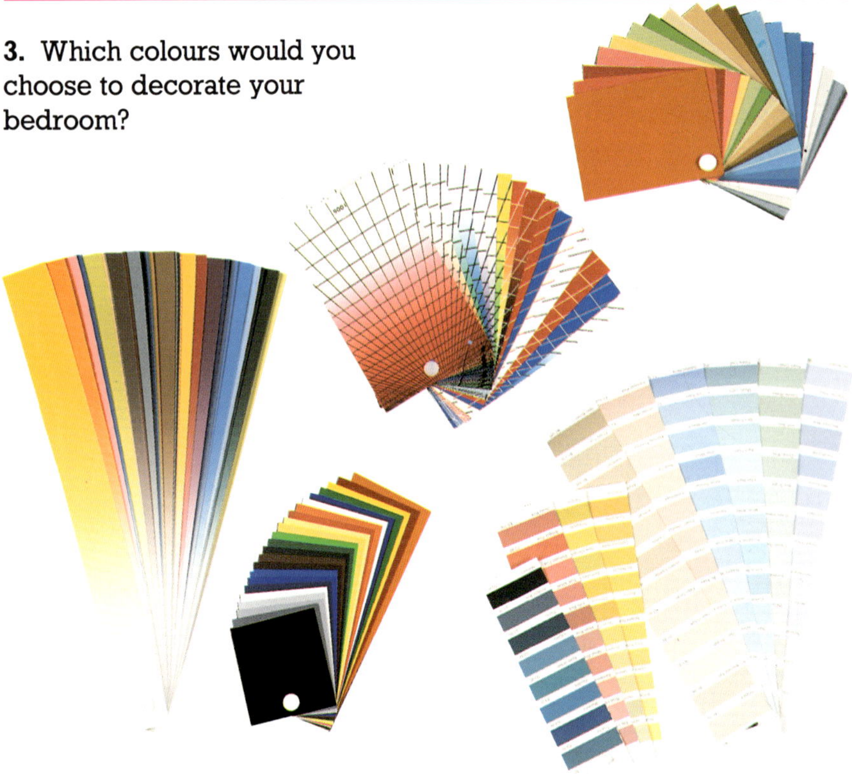

4. Warm colours – and cool colours.

Make a picture using a limited palette.
An icy sea ...
... or tropical sun.

Black and white contrast

You will need: black paper (A4), white paper (A3), a pencil, a ruler, scissors, cold water paste.

1. Fold a sheet of A4 black paper in half. Draw a line from one corner to within 1cm of the top of the fold. Cut out the triangle and cut along the fold. You now have two identical triangles.

2. Keeping the two triangles together, cut away some shapes (triangles, rectangles, semi-circles) from the edges. You may wish to draw them first.

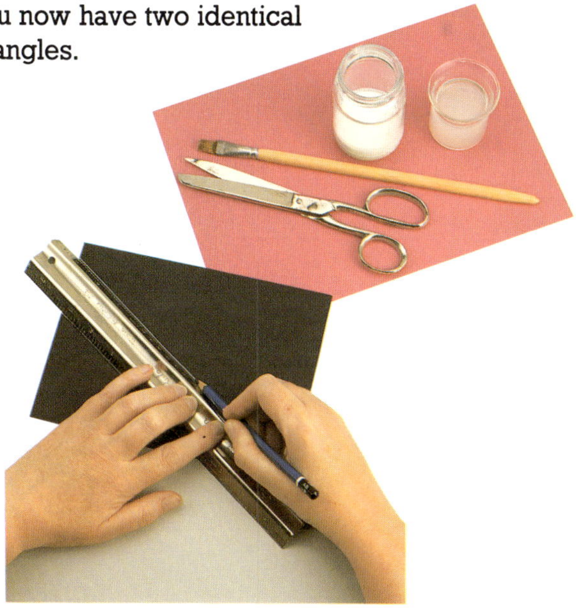

3. Arrange, and then stick, the cut-out shapes on the piece of A3 white paper so that they lie opposite to, and reflect, the spaces from which they were cut.

4. The finished design, showing the sharp contrast between black and white.

FURTHER IDEAS

Rainbow crayons

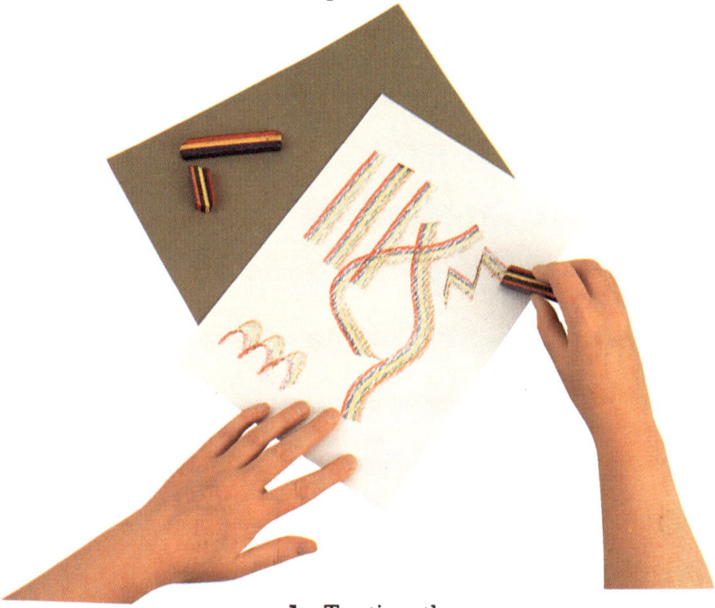

1. Testing the crayons.

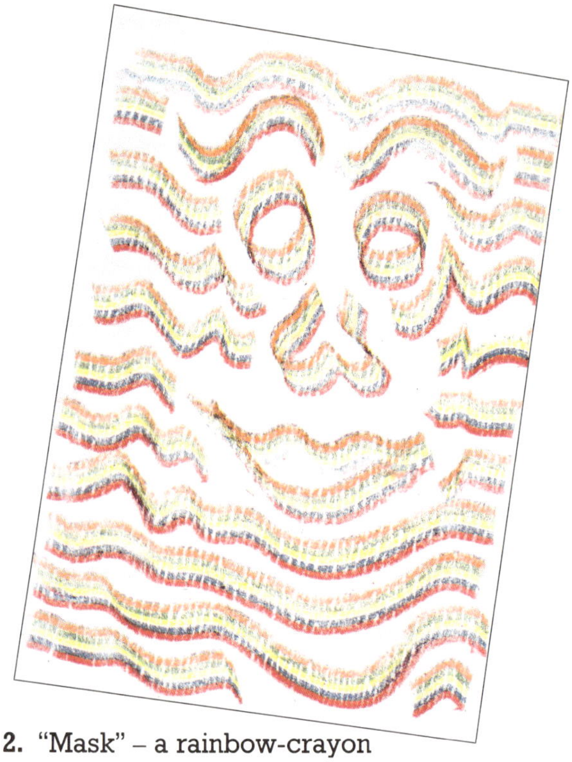

2. "Mask" – a rainbow-crayon design.

Fabric collage

You will need: different scraps of bought printed fabric, some paper, scissors, PVA glue.

The colours used in the bought printed fabrics you have collected are permanent. They do not wash out like your natural dyes. Use your scraps to make a fabric collage.

A photographic study

Use a camera to take photographs of colour in our world. You can begin by using some of the ideas mentioned in each section of this book. Would it be possible to do this with a black-and-white film?

An illustrated dictionary

Make an illustrated dictionary of words which have links with colour. Here are some examples:

colours in feelings: "green with envy", "seeing red".

colours in birds: blackbird, greenfinch;

colours in geography: the Black Forest, the Red Sea;

GLOSSARY

Camouflage
The use of colour by animals and plants to blend into their natural surroundings, so that they are "hidden".

Chromatography
A way of separating different colours.

Colour
The sensation we perceive when light of different wavelengths falls on our eyes.

Colour-blindness
The inability to distinguish between certain colours. People who are colour-blind often cannot tell the difference between red and green.

Colour schemes
Ordered arrangements of colours; for example, in decorating and furnishing a room.

Colour vision
The ability of the human eye to detect differences in the wavelengths of light.

Colour wheel
The colours of the spectrum joined round in a circle or wheel.

Complementary colours
These are opposite each other on the colour wheel.

Dye
A colour or stain used to change the colour of a material. Dyes can be either natural or synthetic (man-made).

Filter
A coloured screen (sometimes made of glass or cellophane) which allows only certain colours to pass through while absorbing others. It filters the light.

Harmonious colours
These are next to each other on the colour wheel.

Medium
A substance which binds the coloured pigment in artists' materials, such as the wax in wax crayons.

Mordant
A chemical substance which fixes the dye in the dyeing process. A mordant makes the colour "fast" so that it will not wash out.

Pigment
Small particles which give the colour to different materials and substances. The colouring matter in paints and dyes.

Primary colours
In light, these are red, green and blue; in paints they are red, yellow and blue.

Refraction
Changing the direction of a beam of light, causing it to break up. When white light is refracted it can produce a spectrum.

Retina
The inside surface of the back of the eye which is sensitive to light. Different cells in the retina are sensitive to red, green and blue light.

Secondary colours
These are produced by mixing two primary colours together. They are yellow, cyan and magenta in light and orange, green and purple in paints.

Spectrum
A coloured band of seven colours: red, orange, yellow, green, blue, indigo, violet. It is caused by the refraction of light. You can see the spectrum in a rainbow.

Tertiary colours
These are produced by mixing two secondary colours together. They are all greyish colours.

Wavelengths
Distances between points on the wave band along which light waves can be measured. The visible spectrum is in the middle wavelengths.

INDEX